WHILE IN FOSTER CARE

BY MARIA I. SOLON
ILLUSTRATED BY CAMERON WILSON

I wake up in a place full of kids like me, we laugh, we play, we get sad and sometimes we get angry...

People may say I have to calm down but they don't know the baggage I carry around.

I move so much I have a lot of friends and I know so many people the surprises never end.

I have been to many schools
and I have been to many cities.

GROCERY STORE

Sometimes I get tired and I just want to watch some TV.

The kids I meet at school tell me about their families and I can't help but wonder how it would be for me.

When I talk to them I pretend
I have a family too, it's not fun
to lie, but it's what I have to do.

I can't sleep because I think about my life all night and how different it would be if I had mine.

I wish I had what others have,
I wish I wasn't me.

If other kids in school only knew what I have been through, they wouldn't be so harsh, they wouldn't be so mean.

BECOME
A FOSTER
PARENT.

I only want love, is that too much to ask? I only want a family that's loves me for me until the end.

I can't wait for that day to come, I hope it comes very soon, I want my forever family and I want it to be true.

www.ingramcontent.com/pod-product-compliance
Lightning Source LLC
Chambersburg PA
CBHW040041240726
48664CB00003B/1019